After Our First
Hello

BARBARA FOURNIER

PAGE PUBLISHING, INC.
New York, NY

First originally published by Page Publishing, Inc. 2017

ISBN 978-1-63568-057-7 (Paperback)
ISBN 978-1-63568-888-7 (Hard Cover)
ISBN 978-1-63568-058-4 (Digital)

Printed in the United States of America

CONTENTS

ACKNOWLEDGMENTS

This book was written with an eye toward having the public acknowledge who we really are as stylists, what we must listen to every day. It has turned into so much more in the three years it took to complete.

I wish to thank Al, my wonderful husband of forty-five years, for your love and support and for encouraging me to write. I thank you for always listening to my daily salon drama, also for lending a hand with my clients when needed. For going above and beyond with them, changing a toilet seat, replacing a wall phone, giving them a ride now and then—all the little things that made a difference in their lives. Most of all I thank you for loving me. You will be my squeeze forever and a day. I love you.

Crystal, our beautiful and intelligent daughter, how can I ever thank you for taking a red pencil to this manuscript without hesitation, not an easy task when it's your mom. For always lending an ear on your long ride home from work every day. For allowing me to write about your life through years, the good and the bad. For encouraging me to move forward with this manuscript when I felt like stopping the whole process. For making me see what I have accomplished in my life and to be proud of it.

Our biggest accomplishment was you. You will forever be our baby girl. I love you.

To Jeff for being an amazing son-in-law and for loving our daughter so deeply. You are a treasure for sure.

To John Gray for his permission to reference his column and for his encouragement on my journey. I truly admire you as a journalist. I thank you.

My sincere thanks to Tracy for reading a few chapters in the beginning of this book and encouraging me to keep writing no matter what happens, for telling me she laughed, cried, and wanted more. Tracy as a stylist you got much more than you bargained for; now you have our daughter Crystal as your client. I thank you for being so good at what you do and my sincerest thanks and love for being her friend. You're the best.

To Pauline Bartel for all your help in class as the instructor on writing and selling your book. For your honesty when reading my manuscript and always being a professional, I thank you from the bottom of my heart.

Also to the rest of my family for taking the time to read and critique this book in its early stages. It helped me to look deeper. My love to all of you.

DISCLAIMER

Although the title of this book sounds like it should be a romance novel with a cover photo of a well-built man with long, flowing hair riding a horse into the sunset, trust me, it is not. It is, however, a collection of short stories from my world as a stylist and much more. This is absolutely the right title as you will see.

The content of this book is based solely on the authors memories. Some identifying details of the individuals and events in the book have been changed to protect their privacy.

INTRODUCTION

For quite some time, I've thought about writing, but the process has been a little daunting. Thoughts came faster than I could put them down on paper. Therefore, nothing made sense. That was until I attended a class on writing and selling your book. The course was given at Hudson Valley Community College in Troy, New York. The instructor for the course, Pauline Bartel, nationally known author and writing consultant (Bartel Communications), said in the very beginning that writing a book can be accomplished if you approach it as if you were eating an elephant. Yes, I said eating an elephant. What she meant was, you can do it if you take one bite at a time. She didn't say how long it would take, but the concept was there. I find I have scrap paper everywhere with thirty- five years of client tales, thoughts on the world we live in, and my ideas on the lack of common sense. Now all I have to do is organize this elephant on my plate. That will take a whole lot of focus and a very hefty appetite.

After Our First Hello was born in my head and in my heart. It has been nurtured by me for thirty-five years, but its first steps were taken only after I took my first step into Ms. Bartel's classroom.

CHAPTER ONE

Blindsided

Never did I think it possible that my cosmetology license would require me to make life-and-death decisions. Nor did I realize that my license was also considered a right for people to confide all of their life's problems to me. A client from many years ago is a very good case in point. His name, well that will remain with me, as with all the others. He is a nice young man with an insatiable love for music. He had incredible insight into all aspects, but first love was guitar. He would talk to me about it as if I really knew to what he was referring. I assure you I did not, but that's okay. His mom would bring him in for his haircuts from time to time, not often enough but that's all right as well. This young man has a disability and relied on her to care for him. She was a sweet woman, very down to earth and easy to talk to. She was never a client, although I wish she would have allowed me to make her feel special even if it was only once. It was obvious she never considered herself a priority. I knew she had a lot on her plate. They had very little in life and I assume he was not easy to handle. Sometimes at the end of a paycheck there is nothing left for you. Money or energy.

I had not seen this young man in a very long time. I had heard at some point that his mom passed away. I don't know who took over his care but I never saw him again. A few years later, I received a phone call from him. I was excited to hear his voice again and asked how he was doing. I just thought that he was ready to be a client once again. He proceeded to tell me that he was going to end it all—his life! I could barely breathe and my heart was pounding. I tried to talk to him calmly, keep him talking but he hung up. I dialed the police. And silently asked that he be okay. After speaking with police later that day, they assured me he was fine. A few hours later I received yet another call from this same young man. I'm expecting him to say thank you for caring but instead he said to me, "You need to mind your own fucking business." (His words, not mine.)

CHAPTER TWO

Salon as a Business

Your hairstylist is one of the most important people in your life. Even if you don't have hair (more on that later). Yet, so often we are portrayed in a much different light. I've never seen a movie or a television show that actually made the hairdresser look intelligent. How sad for all of us in this field. It's not the career that most college graduates choose for their path to wealth and fame. It is, however, a career that requires much more stamina than I could ever have imagined and an education that comes in the form of real-life experience. There is no cap and gown for that.

When I went to school to obtain my license, we were taught the basics—hair color, cutting, blow drying, sets, and styling. What they neglected to teach us was the actual percentages of the business, which I believe is 10 percent know-how and 90 percent knowing how to listen. That's the real world of a stylist.

We are the people who make you look your best for that job interview or that special occasion and we are the professionals that you come to with the most unbelievable tales that anyone could ever imagine. We often find ourselves scratching our heads thinking, why in the world would you leave these stories with us, in our hearts, and in our minds?

Most any stylist will confirm a client will tell you everything about their lives. The reason I believe is the intimate connection the two have. The trust, the closeness—after all, you are definitely hands on. It starts with a shampoo that not only cleanses the hair and scalp, but also relaxes you, like a massage would. It can be almost euphoric. Quite often, all I had to do was ask (first mistake) "How is your day?"

Is this book just my memoirs, a self-help read, a long-winded advice column, or is it my own take on common sense? Quite possibly all the above but I'll let you the reader decide.

CHAPTER THREE

Survival Part I (Just a Little Background)

I often wonder would I have turned out the way I did if I were raised in a house full of happiness and love, something I will never know, and at age sixty-nine, should I care?

I'm one of eight children, the oldest girl. The spoiled one as some would say. My mother doted on me, but not for the reason you would think. You see, I had rheumatic fever at age nine and was bedridden for most of that year. This made it easy to be called "spoiled" because I was waited on a lot. The living room sofa became my new bed. My parents were told to get a private tutor for school (which they couldn't afford). So instead, it was the minister of a local church. He helped as much as he could, but I didn't learn what was required and I had to repeat the third grade anyway the following year.

My father who worked in a steel mill for thirty years passed away in 1969 with steel dust in his lungs. It was awful to watch as he tried to catch his breath.

My mother, I believe, had the hardest job of all. She had to raise all of us on a shoestring budget in a house that had no bathroom and no running water. We did, however, have an out-house that had three holes. I never understood why three, but sometimes it could be a scary place and I was glad to have the company of a sister once in a while. Mom passed away in 1991.

The house we grew up in was located on a country road in a small rural neighborhood. Everyone knew who you were and all about your life, good or bad. The house was a pretty good size, but it was cold and damp. We had a wood stove in the living room with a grate in the ceiling above it to heat the upstairs, but none of it helped much. When my parents could afford it, we'd get a coal delivery. A huge truck would back up to the basement doors and literally pipe in a ton of coal. We would bring it upstairs in metal buckets to put on the fire after the wood was hot enough to ignite the coal. I've wondered whether the coal dust played a role in my dad's breathing problems as well. The kitchen also had a wood and coal stove. I remember mom trying to cook on that thing. In later years, we had propane stoves installed in the kitchen and the living room. Still no central heating system and certainly no insulation in the walls. I can remember at times when my mom and I were wallpapering, you could see through to the outside. Old plaster would fall away from between the slats that formed the walls. For some reason, wallpaper seemed to be one of the few pleasures for her. It was also something we did together, which is a fond memory for me. There were two bedrooms upstairs: boys in one, girls in another. Downstairs was another larger bedroom that was used only in summer months by my parents. The rest of the time rooms were closed off because of the drafty cold air. Just off the living room was a small room that was my parents' bedroom for the winter months. Just to the right was an empty room. Literally empty. Not even a floor. This was to be the bathroom. It was never installed until after my father passed away. Mom once told me that every time an attempt was made to have a bath put in that room, something bad would happen. I never wanted to question just what those bad things were. Still don't. As we grew to be on our own, we wanted to put in the bathroom for Dad (my parents had separated by then), but he wanted no part of it. Don't know why. Even when it was eventually installed in order to sell the house after he died, the plumbing was never hooked up for use, all show. Obviously inspectors weren't used or maybe the new owners didn't care.

There was a lot of fighting when we were young, but I firmly believe it was the alcohol that was the biggest culprit. It really was only when they both drank that the fists started to fly.

I also remember the huge blocks of welfare cheese that we somehow got once in a while, but we were not on welfare.

Wow! That was a flashback. I guess they did the best they could with what life handed them.

Money, well, I can't imagine trying to raise all of us on what they made. Anyway, in spite of how we were brought up or maybe because of how we were brought up, I believe all eight of us turned out to be pretty comfortable with our lives. And yes: I do know that there is a tremendous number of people who had it worse and still have it worse than we did growing up, but when you are young, your world is the only one that matters.

I was long gone from home when my parents separated but they never divorced. She had met someone else, and after Dad passed away, she married this man. They eventually moved to Florida. At least she had someone with her and a whole new life, experiencing new things with new friends. She remained in Florida until he died suddenly of an aneurism. Soon after, she became very forgetful, wandering into a different town, not knowing where she was, trying to call me at a telephone number of a salon I hadn't worked at in a very long time. Thankfully, one of the stylists there remembered her and called me. It was time to do something. My sister and I flew to get her and bring her home. Big change in her in a short period of time. I don't believe anyone in the family could have handled her, the changing moods—one minute she hugged, you the next she was ready to hit you. She came to stay with me for a while and then at my sister's home. My husband and I were asleep one night, and at some odd hour, he gave me a shove to wake me. There she was standing over him just staring. I said to her, "Mom, what's wrong. Why aren't you in bed?" That's when she began yelling at me, calling me every name in the book, telling me I was no good. Between the two of us, we managed to get her back to bed. Whew! A wide awake nightmare. What happened to being the favorite daughter, and what had happened to my mom? I don't ever remember feeling so helpless. I started to cry.

It seemed inevitable what the next step would be. My sister (thank God for her strength) took care of all the arrangements for her to be placed in a nursing facility. That's a tremendous amount of work to keep track of everything—attorneys, doctors, and financial part as well, i.e., selling her home. At the time I had my hands full with the new salon, and that's no excuse for throwing it all on my sister. As prepared as I am for life's curve balls, that's something that was just too much for my heart to handle.

CHAPTER FOUR

Abuse

Abuse—whether it is substance, mental, or physical—is a nightmare for everyone you know. Common sense goes right out the window when either one is present.

During my years as a stylist, I've seen abuse in several forms. No matter the situation, it's not an easy conversation to have when the abused is sitting in my chair. One client in particular didn't tell me right away, but I knew by the attempt at make-up to cover the bruises on her face and sleeves that weren't long enough to cover the black-and-blue arms.

These women would tell me stories of how they didn't get along with their spouses at all. They had very different views on everything, which seemed to be the case with all of the victims. Whether it was the raising of their children, even which places they should work or different types of studies they were working on at the time. It seemed these women were never right in making choices. I'd say there was only one wrong choice, staying with the abuser for so long. I never met these men and so glad that I didn't. Many times I asked the question, why not leave? Money was not a problem for a few of them. There was always an excuse. It's not the right time, or our daughter is getting married soon. Next time was our son is moving and I need to help him. With any kind of abuse, there is always an excuse that is until you just can't take it anymore. Hopefully that time will come before someone gets seriously hurt or dies. One of the saddest excuse was "my husband is sick right now." Sick? Are you kidding me? He's sick in more ways than you know, lady. I would have hit him with a baseball bat in his sleep!

Another victim told me, "I can't leave. I have never had a job and now we are getting older and the abuse is more mental than physical." What do you say to that?

I would get phone calls at home from some of these women once in a while. They just wanted to talk. Sometimes alcohol was involved, which can play a huge part in this entire scenario but still not a reason for hitting someone. There never needs to be a reason when you are the abuser. I would listen carefully for any signs that these women might be in trouble. When they got tired, they hung up and I'm the one that had the sleepless night.

Is there a fear of maybe being alone or having to explain your life to someone? Having people judge you? Things seemed to quiet down shortly after I retired. I'm guessing in one instance because of his illness. One gave up her career and is now working in a field that does not require the education that she worked so hard to obtain. How sad for her and for anyone who may have been helped by her achievements.

Whether these women were highly educated, financially secure, middle class or not, didn't seem to matter. To me common sense should have prevailed, but it did not.

I understood abuse having watched my parents beat each other up after a night out drinking. The difference of course, where was my mom supposed to go? There were no shelters back then, certainly no money either. Her mother told her you make your bed you lie in it. Eight children, no money, and the important thing to remember here is no emotional support from anyone and no education in order to find a better-paying job. So things were different for my mom's generation and yet exactly the same in so many ways.

There will always be families that need a way to survive abuse, but now there are programs out there that are supposed to offer aid and comfort. For some of these women it may be their status in town that keeps them from seeking the support needed. In others maybe the feeling of failure in their marriage or possibly just plain fear of the unknown.

Like I said in the beginning, abuse is a nightmare no matter how you look at it. I felt the pain in my heart with these clients, just like I did with my mom. In all cases I could do nothing about it. A very smart gentleman who was trying to teach me relaxation techniques once told me, "You cannot be a bandage for the world." Wouldn't it be nice if I could?

CHAPTER FIVE

The Fear of Hair

Almost from day one of my career, I knew this woman would be a loyal client. She followed me wherever I went to work. She was always nice to me and very generous. It's hard to write about her. I think it's because she was with me for so long and we shared our life experiences for all of those years that it's hard to know where to start.

I guess maybe with the absolute fear she had when it came to her hair. It may seem odd in today's world of styling, but if you look back to the seventies and earlier, you didn't wash your hair every day like a lot of us do today. If you were lucky enough to go to a salon, it was once a week. Her hair was her nemesis.

Of course this is a plus for any stylist. It means a steady weekly client, which is rare these days. Most younger clients come only when a cut is needed. She was young when we met and told me that getting her hair done once a week was her own little indulgence, and to me, she deserved this treat. Actually we all should treat ourselves better. I will never forget in the early years with this client, having to do her hair before she went into the hospital. Why get your hair done when they're just going to mess it up with a lovely paper hat in the OR? I was scared to death. Everything frightened me. I was brand-new to the business and she was in labor.

She would tell me that she sometimes purchased her clothing from a catalog so she wouldn't have to mess her hair in a dressing room while trying things on. She didn't want to pull clothing over her head and it was easier to maneuver at home. Oh well, I guess we all have our little idiosyncrasies.

I had asked her many times if she would allow me teach her how to take care of it during the week but to no avail. Strange how something that seemed so easy, for me anyway, would completely baffle someone as smart as she was. You know what? Now that I think about it, there is no way in hell that I ever could do her job either.

We shared a lot of life's ups and downs, families, careers, illnesses, and everything in between, but nothing, not even breast cancer, ever frightened her as much as her hair at least to my knowledge. Another thing to note, she never did lose her hair during cancer treatment. How do you suppose she would have handled that mess, or for that matter, how do you think I would have handled her during that mess?

She really was a fantastic client. Not many people stay with the same stylist for your whole career. It was difficult to say good-bye to her when I retired and she wanted to stay in touch after but I had to let her go like I did the rest of my clients for my own wellbeing. I did call her and explain why I had to reboot my life and she understood completely. I thank her for being so understanding. I'm sure she knows who she is in this book venture of mine, even without the name. A little side note to her: Love you.

CHAPTER SIX

Alzheimer's Disease

This might be the most difficult topic to put on paper; I have a real personal connection. My mother had Alzheimer's. I think it is one of the cruelest diseases out there. I can't imagine how lost you must feel when this first stage rears its ugly head. Trying to remember smaller things in the beginning—things like misplacing an item, forgetting to take a medication once in a while, or wearing an outfit that you normally wouldn't put together. These are things that we most often brush off as part of getting older. But then comes the feeling of being completely lost. I can't comprehend the fear my mom must have felt not knowing people, not even her own children. Also, not knowing why these people were leaving her in a strange place (nursing home).

"Why don't they know I can't escape from my blurred mind and my wavering body?"

She would walk and walk up and down the nursing home halls constantly. I'm guessing she was looking for a way out of this world. I hated the blank stare on her face as the disease progressed. The stressed look from not knowing how to communicate with anyone. My heart was broken. I had no way of helping her. Every once in a while, I would see a glimmer of recognition in her, that she might know who I was, but those moments were not nearly enough for me. I often feel that this woman had to struggle in life, and how sad that she also had to struggle to die. She had that dreadful disease for at least eight years. Not fair at all. I was the last relative to see her before she passed away. As I was leaving the nursing home that day, I had a strange feeling come over me. I turned myself around and went back to kiss her good-bye again. I guess I somehow knew it would be our last.

This brings me to my next client.

CHAPTER SEVEN

A Kind Soul

She was one of the friendliest, kind-hearted, and funniest people I know. Who wouldn't want a client or friend like her?

This lady worked with one of my dearest relatives. My cousin mentioned I was a hairdresser and that's how I came to know her. She would come to the salon once a month for her haircuts or for perms every once in a while. Steady loyal customer. When my cousin became ill with cancer, she needed to use all of her sick time because of the disease and she soon ran out. That's when this kind woman took it upon herself to donate her own comp time to my cousin. Believe me, it was appreciated. Unfortunately, my cousin passed away.

This client continued to come to the salon. She lived a good distance away, so this had to be an inconvenience for her. I have to say she is one of the few clients that didn't convey all her problems to me. For this I was grateful. We could talk about everything from the latest movie to the next big name in politics. This was a really nice change of pace for me.

I had begun to see a change in her a few years later. She was not keeping herself as neat as she once did. Her personality changed, all the signs that I did not want to see in this person or any other for the rest of my life. She came to the salon one day crying her heart out. She had been driving around for hours looking for me. She was so afraid she had missed her appointment; she didn't have one.

I calmed her down, telling her she wasn't late, finished the client in my chair, and then set her hair and put her under the dryer. I then contacted a family member to make them aware of what had happened and how this and other recent changes in her concerned me. I asked that someone come to pick her up and drive her car home. No way was I about to let her go home by herself. One of the responses I got was "There is nothing wrong with her. She just doesn't pay attention and watches too much television."

What the f . . . ?

Anyway they came to get her. The conversation didn't go well when they arrived. They yelled at her and told her there was no reason she couldn't drive home. Mind you, this poor woman had no idea that I'm the one that said she shouldn't drive home. Who knows where she might have gone next. I finally had it with their stupid comments and I told them enough. I was very close to calling someone like the police or some sort of social services. I then told them they needed to find a salon closer to home for her to go to. I then kissed her, hugged her, and thanked her for being a wonderful client all these years and that I would miss her. I said good-bye and made damn sure someone else got in the driver's seat.

All I kept thinking was, how far do I go? Did I want another episode like the disabled client who wanted to kill himself? I chalked this up to another case of no common sense. These children were in their forties, not teenagers. I ask you, the reader, how would you have handled this situation? Not easy, is it? I know in my heart that I was right to call her family, but not so sure they were the right family members to call.

CHAPTER EIGHT

Young at Heart

In all my years as a stylist, I don't think I ever saw a woman with the amount of energy as this next client. She was so full of life, so fun loving, and always looking for a new day to hold onto.

This lovely woman was a dancer. I'm very sure that's what kept her so young for so long. She too was a client from the early days of my career, a treat to have in any salon.

She lost her husband at a very young age, before I met her. She later had a gentleman that she was pretty tight with but never even considered another go at marriage. There truly was only one love for her, the first. Not that she didn't enjoy her other men—she certainly did!

She was one of those women who had white hair at a very young age, which in some cases makes you look old. Not her. Maybe part of the reason was her personality. Whatever the reason, she was one of the few that I never even considered trying to change her hair color.

Dancing, I believe became the reason for her existence. I envied the excitement that filled her whenever she would order a new dance outfit; you know the ones with the short ruffled skirts with the ruffled panties to match. I would tease her relentlessly about showing the men her undies when she twirled. I just loved to hear her shy giggle.

It seemed like all of a sudden she began to fail right out of the blue, when in fact it really had been coming on for quite some time. I just didn't want it to be so.

She had children that lived in another state, and for many years, she would drive there alone. This always frightened the hell out of me as she aged, but she did it for as long as she could without incident. She had a good relationship with the kids from what I could see anyway.

I called one of them with my concerns over things that began to go wrong. Things like her personality and lapses in memory. All of her issues became really noticeable after her gentleman friend moved away to be near family because of his failing health and later passed away. This was quite a blow for her.

As time went on she would tell me things that certainly disturbed me. Things like her mechanic putting tires on her car when in fact she had new ones put on the year before. The only place she went at this point was to church, the grocery store, and to see me. New tires my ass! I notified one of the children. The response, "Oh well, she's getting forgetful." What? I would have sued that guy in a heartbeat. I hate when our senior citizens get taken advantage of so easily, especially now that I am one. Don't you think they should have at least inquired about it, make the guy sweat a little?

Another incident was crazy. She told me her homeowner's insurance policy was going to be canceled unless she had the roof replaced. Seriously? The roof still had some years left on it. Thank goodness her neighbor was on top of this one. She told me that he suggested she contact her local agent and find out what is going on. The agent told her that the insurance companies were going around house to house making sure roofs were kept up so they would not have to pay unnecessary claims. This I could understand, but when it's not needed, it's not needed. Her neighbor told her to tell the agent that she was going to call the main office to find out if this was true. The agent immediately said, "I'll call the main office to see what we can do." Bull! He didn't have time to make that call. He called her right back and said that they were going to renew her policy for another year. My first thought, maybe the agent had a relative that was a roofer. I just told her to thank the neighbor.

Holidays are a tough time for a great many seniors—families live far away, or things just happen in life that cause their children to be . . . how do I say this? Maybe less interested in what's going on with mom and dad. Whatever the reason, it breaks my heart. I have seen this so many times in my career. This same client once told me she would be staying home for the holidays. She could no longer drive the distance and no one was coming to get her. You would think that one of the family members could have made arrangements to get her, whether it is one of the grandchildren or a bus ticket or even come to spend the day with her for that matter. Like I always say, I do not know the family dynamics, but this really bothered me. Anyway, Al and I asked my client to come with us for the holiday, but of course, she said no. I would have said the same thing. That year she let a friend talk her into going to the senior's center with her for Christmas dinner. She told me never again; it was the most depressing day ever. On the plus side of things, she never did think of herself as a senior citizen. How great is that?

When this lovely lady passed away, her children came to take care of her funeral arrangements and clean out her house so it could be put it on the market to sell. One of the children came into the salon to get a haircut before the funeral. I wanted to shave this person's head for not being with her that Christmas, but I remained a professional. Maybe it was my own guilt creeping in, not wanting to believe that I may have been a negligent daughter at times.

CHAPTER NINE

Survival Part II: You, Me, and Baby Girl

My husband, Al, and I started our journey together three thousand miles from home. It was a challenge, to say the least. He was drafted into the army—yes, way back when they still had the draft. He was sent to the state of Washington to be deployed to Vietnam. I thank God that he never had to go. They began to bring the troops home from the war or conflict whatever they called it back then, so we spent the remaining time that he had to serve in Tacoma, Washington. The base was Fort Lewis. I have to say that living so far from home was at times difficult but the best thing that could happen to a newly married couple. We had to figure things out on our own. There was no way either one of us could run to mommy or daddy if we had a spat.

Whatever problems arose we dealt with it one thing at a time. I think that all couples should consider this just for a short time while you both really get to know about each other. Warts and all!

Our daughter Crystal was born while we were there. Talk about a challenge! There was no family around; no baby showers to count on either. Her baby clothes I purchased at a garage sale including cloth diapers. Remember when? We lived in an efficiency apartment. That means the only inside door was to the bathroom (at least I had a bathroom). The rest was living, kitchen, and bedroom all in one. Good thing I was raised the way that I was—it helped. The unit was furnished with sofa, kitchen table and chairs, and a bed. I purchased two hot and cold cups, two spoons, one of which was a grapefruit spoon, and an aluminum sauce pan all at the same garage sale. We would have cereal first then wash out the cups to have instant coffee.

Our daughter had stomach issues for the first six months of her life. I don't know how we stood the constant crying, especially my husband who had to be on base in the wee hours of the morning. I think the only time she didn't cry was when she went to the pediatrician; there she would be all giggles. I would tell the doctor about the screaming and she said, "Not this little darling." She told me she was colic. Now get this, she suggested I put her in a room that had a door we could close and let her cry. As I mentioned, the only room with a door in the apartment was the bathroom. I couldn't leave my new baby in the bathroom! The doctor also said to give her a tablespoon of good scotch in her formula. She claimed that as long as she was fed and dry and no gas, the scotch might help relax her. Don't you think *I* should have taken the scotch? Today, I probably would be in big trouble for such a thing. She also suggested that we move into a place with a door. We took her advice and soon moved into a mobile home park near the base.

Our precious little girl was a year old when I returned to New York. I came with our daughter to find an apartment before Al was discharged. It wasn't easy. We had to move in with Al's parents for a few weeks, which was a little uncomfortable since they never really cared for me after we announced we were getting married. I am a bit older than my husband and that didn't set well with them. My husband soon followed and we did find an apartment—not the nicest place—but it was home for a while.

Al went to work for the post office, remained there for thirty-four years. He was diagnosed with prostate cancer, and decided that after the surgery, it was time to retire from that stressful career. I am so grateful that he is well and now works at a desk for the state of New York with people who appreciate him every day.

I went to cosmetology school and started my career in 1976; I'm now sixty-nine years old, soon to hit seventy. Wow!

Al and I have been married for forty-five years. Wonder where those years went at times. Our daughter Crystal is the light in our lives; she is a graduate of a college in western New

York, has a career, and is married for nearly eighteen years to a terrific young man, Jeff, whom we love and adore. No children and that is their choice. That's the way it should be, their choice not ours.

We are truly blessed to have Crystal in our lives. She always makes sure we see her at least once a week. We go on vacations with her and Jeff once a year, sometimes twice, and most important she loves her father and me as much as we love and adore her. What more could you ask of someone?

CHAPTER TEN

The Breast-Feeder

Why is it that some people feel they should be on display all the time? Their children are put there as well. Is it necessary to parade your children around the social media track?

I will admit I am not on social media yet, but I'm quite sure I will be soon. Right now I fear it. It alarms me to think a total stranger, or someone with mental issues, could know everything there is to know about you and your children because we have a need to show the world everything we do.

Have you ever wondered where this may have started? We used to send photos of each other and our loved ones through the mail; by that I mean the USPS, not e-mail. We could document the family functions by creating photo albums. I see now a resurgence of cameras. I'm glad about that. We need to stop putting ever part of us on display. Which somehow brings me to this client. Maybe it's a little food for thought.

Now here is a tale off the client list that may seem to be taken way out of context for the times. Please remember, and I'm guessing, that about 70 percent of my clientele were seniors and most had very old-school ways of thinking. Then again my own way of thinking is the same as theirs at times. This all happened back when I opened my first salon.

One of the girls that worked in the salon had a client come in with her two children. The little girl was getting her hair cut. The child wasn't the problem; it was the mother. She decided to breastfeed her infant son while in the waiting area of the salon. One of my clients was under a hair dryer at the time and was very embarrassed and uncomfortable by this display. I asked the woman if she would like to go into the break room to feed her baby. You would have thought that I asked her to jump off a bridge or something. She proceeded to tell me, "Breast-feeding is a very natural thing to do." My response, "So is peeing, lady, but I really have no desire to pull down my pants and do it in the middle of my salon.

I never saw her again. Ask me if I care?

What the hell happened to respect for seniors and also what the hell happened to manners in general? I know breast-feeding is natural and I know what I said back to her wasn't very professional, but sometimes you just have to . . . well, you know.

CHAPTER ELEVEN

Not the Children, the Parents

In a salon a child, whether brand-new to the world or teenagers, can be a nightmare. Let me re-phrase that. Mothers who bring in their small children for haircuts are the nightmares. Teenagers are a nightmare on any given day, time, or place. That I have come to see as a rite of passage.

It is very normal for moms and grandmas to want to record every single moment in their little darling's life. But, and that's a big but, please use some common sense when you bring your children into a salon. I can't begin to tell you how unnerving it is to try and cut a little one's hair while a camera is on top of me. Take a few shots and sit down. Stop hovering. The child is screaming and you are saying, "Oh, isn't she cute?" Yes, your child is cute. All kids are cute when they are little at least, but you are a pain in my ass. The child is sitting in a chair with a strange woman coming at them trying to put a cape around their neck and scissors to their head. Did you expect them to smile for the camera? This is a very serious situation. This is extremely dangerous for your child and for the stylist. Also there is another thing you should know: a child's haircut shouldn't be cheaper than an adult's. It is so much harder to cut a moving target.

CHAPTER TWELVE

A Journalist after My Own Heart

John Gray is a journalist in our area who writes a weekly column for *The Record* and the *Saratogian*, both newspapers in upstate New York. It's called very appropriately "Fade to Gray." He is also an anchor on a local ABC/Fox 23 news program, and one other important note . . . he's an Emmy winner. I've long admired this man's column and look forward to one day meeting him in person, which I'm sure I will have to do soon or I will be in trouble for not getting the proper releases to write about him or to reference his column.

One of the articles he wrote was about the giving of trophies to grade school children at the end of the season for every sport. Mr. Gray asked the question "At what age should it stop?" There are a lot of ideas out there on the subject I'm sure. His view was to stop when children's ages reach double digits. My feeling is that we are doing these children an injustice. Like Mr. Gray said, "Should we be rewarding them for not winning the game? Should we be rewarding them for, in some cases, not even showing up for practice?"

I say maybe the coach and parents should just stick to taking them for ice cream after the game.

The point is, how can we as parents feel we have done our job if we have not prepared our children for what life is about to hand to them. You must work hard for those rewards. You must learn team work and you must learn that sometimes you win, sometimes you lose but you don't always get the trophy, the raise, the bonus or the promotion. That, in a nutshell, is life! It's a valuable lesson. We need less instant gratification.

I don't know when the change in how parents think happened. I don't understand why a lot of our children who are now in their forties and younger feel the need to please, the need to give, and the need to insist that their child deserves the utmost attention and rewards for doing very little to deserve it and also for showing no respect for the person giving it to them. Mind blowing to say the least.

In my salon I've watched in horror as children not only talked back to their parents but actually yell at them and, in some cases, punch them as well, all while the parent is promising to take them to the toy store or buy them a video game if they sit still. Do you believe these children deserve a trophy? The parents allowed this behavior and I don't know why. I'm a true believer that most children don't want to be this way but just haven't been taught anything different. That's why we need to stop giving these children rewards for doing little or nothing. I think they need structure in their lives. We are the parents, not their friends. They need someone to say no and then explain why. Over the years I've said to our own daughter "because I said so that's why." That's not right either I guess but the point was made. One other thing I told her along the way was that you don't have to like me, you don't even have to love me, but you do have to respect me. That's a rule I will always enforce.

Can you imagine what our armed forces would be without rules, without structure, and without respect? I've said many times those who serve in the military, male or female, are well rounded and can manage without mommy and daddy coddling them. I believe that most are stronger for having been trained in real life, with far more real life experiences. Yes, our soldiers get ribbons and medals, but you can bet that they earned every one of them. A big thank you to all of them.

Oh, and one other thing, I did get the release from Mr. Gray along with a little advice. Thank you, John. I also thank you for wishing me good luck with this writing adventure of mine.

CHAPTER THIRTEEN

Just My Way of Thinking

You get married, you have children, and hopefully, you will teach those children to be self-sufficient, have manners, and respect for other people. That should be your job as a parent.

I know people go ballistic when I say that in our home my husband has always come first and then our daughter. They are shocked. My response to them is that if I do my job right, my daughter will become that self-sufficient, educated person, leave our home and be a happy, well-rounded person who is and always will be loved by both of us.

When your children are out of the house, who are you going to spend the rest of your life with? It's just you and your spouse. If both spouses are not nurturing your relationship all along, putting each other first, then guess what? You will have nothing in later years. Remember, your focus on each other will set an example and teach your child the importance of finding a partner that they can love and trust to always have your back. You won't have to re-learn how to be with just one another. That connection will already be there.

It worked for us. Crystal found a wonderful young man and I hope we had something to do with that. Not to say there weren't a few frogs along the way, but sometimes you have to kiss a few of those to find a prince.

CHAPTER FOURTEEN

It's Not Rocket Science

Sometimes people live in a world of sunshine and lollipops with no idea of what the real meaning of a partnership should be.

I once had a client who held a very prominent position in her field of expertise. Just about every time she came into the salon, she would tell me how hard it was to get the children off to school and to all their extra activities, before and after school and on weekends as well. They were in music, ballet, and all kinds of sports. It was from morning till night. This wasn't the only client with this same dilemma. From what my daughter tells me, this occurs in almost all families now no matter what walk of life. I don't know how these children manage to do homework with those schedules. The father, I believe, was an executive for a large company, so both, I assume, were under a lot of stress.

One day she mentioned that she and her husband were having problems; they just weren't connecting. Is it possible that a person who listens to her client's day after day, trying to figure out where every nut and bolt fits into the building of a home, could not know what's missing in her life? I once said to her, "How can you possibly connect with him if the both of you are running these children in different directions? There is no room for the two of you." I often wonder, are these activities really for the children or are they a status thing for the parents. I understand that keeping the children busy keeps them out of trouble and I know how scared parents are during these times of over-the-top drug use and gangs. I certainly wouldn't want to be raising a child at this time. It just seems like a solution to these new nightmares has to be somewhere. Maybe one parent needs to be home after school instead of sending them off to an activity. Maybe it's time we not rely on an after-school program to care for our children. At least not all the time. Two incomes are usually a must I understand that as well as any parent, but at what cost to the well-being of the whole family?

I continued our conversation by telling her about my husband always coming first. You have to make time for each other. The children will find a way to get to some of these things on their own. Another parent, perhaps, or drop one of these after-school programs.

Anyway she came back for her next appointment and said that she and her husband were planning a night once a week just for the two of them. How long do you think that will last?

I hope the rest of their lives and only get better. Sometimes I think I need a different career title on my door and a paycheck to go with it.

CHAPTER FIFTEEN

I'm Not a Caretaker (Or Am I?)

I can't really remember how or when the relationship with this couple began, but I'm truly grateful to have known the both of them. She too was a woman of great knowledge as was her husband. They ran an investment business for a great many years. They traveled all over the world and would tell me about each trip in full detail. It's sometimes nice to see places through another person's eyes. They really liked being with each other, which to me is very sweet and rare after all those years of marriage. They were both in their eighties. They would bring me gifts from different countries once in a while, which I was thankful for but also felt awkward accepting. I remember they once took a trip to Paris and returned with a beautiful piece of gold jewelry for me. I can't imagine what it cost. I was thrilled with it. I lost it on the golf course while out with my husband one weekend. We drove back to see if we could find it, but as much as we searched, even in near darkness, it was gone. If it was found, no one ever turned it in. I was heartbroken and very disappointed in myself for not being more careful with it. I certainly shouldn't have worn it there.

I did this couples' hair for a very long time, and through those years, I'd gotten to know a lot about them. They spent a great deal of time alone even on the trips they took. I would have thought that they would have made friends along the way other than business acquaintances. They even preferred to dine alone on these adventures. It seemed strange to me but what do I know?

When they started to get to a point where things were going wrong with their health I went into, I have to fix everything in the world mode I guess you would say. He was diagnosed with diabetes, which is something I am familiar with having had it for quite a few years now and he had other health issues as well. I continued to cut his hair but now I was doing it at their home.

Their children, once again, lived in a different state but not really that far away. They rarely visited and the excuses why they didn't seem so lame to me, but this couple always defended them. I say all the time no one knows what went on in child-rearing years but I guess I just can't wrap my head around why they wouldn't be there for the both of them. Maybe I'm making them out to be better parents than they were, I don't know. It did bother me though. I do know these children were given a great deal over the years.

She called me one day at the salon to tell me she couldn't get her husband out of bed. He was weak and disoriented. I told her to call 911 and to check his blood sugar if she could and also give him some orange juice if he needed it. I left the salon and drove like a maniac to her house. She didn't call 911. He was up in his chair and drinking juice. He seemed perfectly fine. I asked what his blood sugar was and she told me they couldn't figure out how the meter worked. Do you believe this? I showed them how to use it, told him he should at least call a doctor, scolded them both for not calling 911, and went back to work. Don't you think that they should have called for some real help and not the hairdresser? This kind of thing happened a lot in my career. I just never knew when or where to draw the line.

Not long after that incident, my husband and I came home from a morning outing and I noticed I had a missed call on my cell phone. It was the wife. I just knew something was wrong. I returned the call and no one answered. I told my husband we needed to get to their house as soon as possible. I went to the door, no answer. I knew her husband didn't leave the house anymore at that point, so I knew something bad happened. I went to the neighbors only to find that the husband had passed away during the night and his wife was at the funeral home with him. I asked if one of the children were with her and the neighbor said that they were coming as soon as they could. I was very upset at his passing and really pissed off with the children. I really don't know why I was so angry, except maybe I thought one of them should have lived closer to help them. Like any of this was my business. I know I will forever regret not insisting my own mom move back from Florida soon after her husband passed.

When I arrived at the funeral home, I told the funeral director who I was and he asked me to come in and speak with the wife. I was relieved to see the son and the daughter sitting with her at the desk. I quickly hugged her and told her I was sorry for her loss and also felt bad that I didn't get her message earlier and then I left.

When everything was over, they decided that the house was too big for her so she went into assisted living—not near her children. This woman had very few friends around to visit with her that I was aware of anyway. Everyone in her old neighborhood was getting on in years, and like I said before, they were kind of loners anyway. The place was beautiful but I think it would have been nicer if they arranged for her to move closer to family. "Barb can come and visit you here." Really? Are they going to leave me to continue looking out for her? I did go to visit and even had lunch with her a few times, but then realized, this was not my responsibility. After some time went by, she did make a few friends to have dinner with and I gradually eased out of her life.

I know that we raise our children to be on their own and to make a life for themselves wherever that may be. I also know it's about making choices and remembering who got you where you are today, who helped you throughout that journey. I'm guessing eighty to ninety percent of the time it was a parent. Whether it was because of them or in spite of them, let's not forget mom and dad.

CHAPTER SIXTEEN

Destination Beauty Show

Now here is something that everyone should experience just once in their lifetime. It's bad enough to have a salon full of stylists with attitude, now add a big city to the mix. Imagine thousands of hairdressers from around the world in one building all trying to see the same show. There were very few exhibits that I could learn from or use in the real world of everyday hairdressing in upstate New York, but watching the people, now that's a show in itself. I often felt like I paid to attend a comedy show. The stylists on stage were so over-the-top bizarre. Their models' hair were sticking out in all directions and I mean hair that was twelve inches, maybe longer, sticking right out, top, sideways, back. Holy crap! When they are trying to demonstrate a haircut you just have to laugh, the scissors and the hair are flying all over the place. It's like they would toss the hair in the air and whatever landed between the blades is what got cut. I wonder if the models had to sign a release of some sort stating that whatever the stylist decided to do on stage was okay. Hmm!

Of course all the various companies are trying to promote their products as well. Most of the time I couldn't afford the wholesale price. How in hell do I push this stuff to a client? This is the reason I'm not rich. I have a hard time telling a person they need something that they don't. I don't mind charging people for my talent as a stylist, but I do have issues with all the sales stuff. If your hair needs some extra help, then that's a different story. Plus, there are so many products on the market. I'd have to spend most of my waking hours on researching the how, what, and why of each one. That takes I believe much more patience than I had at the time.

Probably one of the strangest things I saw at one of these shows was a demonstration on waxing. Remember, this particular show was way back. I'm guessing early 1980s. There she was, a beautiful young model lying naked on a table with everything sticking out for the whole world to see, hair being ripped out like two women in a bar brawl on a Saturday night. No part of the body was off limits. Hot wax being brushed on and hair yanked out. Ouch! This didn't seem to bother the model. Not too much anyway. It was the first time I had seen someone nearly naked at one of these shows. I'm certainly not pure as the driven snow, but I have to admit this shocked the hell out of me. To this day, I have never even considered including waxing as part of my list of services in the salon. Thank goodness there are professionals that do this all the time; it's just not for me. You really have to be a strong person to make this a career choice.

Can you imagine me bringing any of these ideas to my little rural America salon? I can't! Especially considering the percentage of my clientele that were senior citizens. Although when I think about it, there were a few clients that would have fit right in with these people. Like the one that would wear lipstick that covered her lips and beyond (more about her in a minute) or the one that wanted her hair teased so it would look fuller (yeah, that isn't happening; you have to have hair to start with). Oh, and the ones that wanted a rinse on their white hair—why did it always have to be blue? Believe me, it doesn't always look less yellow with a blue rinse—it's blue!

No. You cannot imagine the sights at one of these big-time hair shows from the booths to the demonstrations to the final runway show at the end.

There is wild hair, exotic clothes, and really loud music. You've got feathers and sequins and beads. Oh my! An experience to last a lifetime.

I have to admit the local hair shows were pretty good and I always felt that if you learned just one thing at any of them, it was worth the price of a ticket. Thank goodness for local. It is nice to bring new ideas back to the salon from one of these shows. A lot of times you learned the latest trends, the current hairstyles, or what popular TV or movie star style was hot at the time. I think a lot of hairdressers got really tired of the Farrah

Fawcett look. Can't begin to tell you how many people wanted that haircut. It got to be a joke at the salon, because there is no way in hell some of these women were ever going to look like Farrah! We are, after all, beauticians, not magicians. The other celebrity style was the Dorothy Hamill. Everyone, including my own daughter, had that haircut. Seriously though, thank you to those women, if it weren't for them and all the style maker women before and after them, we would be a boring community of really high bouffant hair. Who knows, we might have the high hair again one day; trends do keep going in circles. Remember short shorts and pedal pushers became hot pants and capris. Or maybe it was the other way around I don't know. Regardless I would certainly be out of business long ago without new ideas or old ones made new again.

CHAPTER SEVENTEEN

Lips and Sips

Over the years there have been a few people that came into the salon that were—let's just say, less than normal, whatever the hell that is these days. Some were my clients; others were clients of the other stylists in the salon, but they were entertaining none the less. One person that jumps to mind is "Lips." We all have some things, quirks you might say, about us that others may think of as odd. That's the only word that comes to mind with this person. Odd. She painted her lips on like a clown. The lipstick was always bright red and drawn on far beyond the natural outline of her lips. It of course was smeared on her teeth too. I know she must have had some issues, but would you let your mother or perhaps your wife or daughter go out in public like that? Someone must have seen this behavior. I do know she was married at the time. Can't imagine what he thought or even if he cared about the way she looked. The other problem . . . she was a kleptomaniac. Not the kind you would think. She only stole my toilet tissue every time she came to the salon. She would disappear into the bathroom for long periods of time and come out with her stretch pants bulging like she all of sudden grew three sizes. I finally had to only place a small amount in the bathroom when I knew she was coming. I would've gone broke feeding her toilet paper habit! I often wondered what kind of illness she had that would cause her to steal just toilet tissue. Believe it or not, when she spoke she seemed very normal and could carry on a perfectly good conversation with anyone.

She never did ask why there wasn't more tissue in the bathroom; perhaps she got the hint. The mind is a tricky little thing, wouldn't you say?

Next up was a situation that was funny as hell but also could have gotten me into a whole lot of trouble.

During the holiday season we used to serve wine and cheese, also coffee and cookies, to the customer's all as a thank you for coming to our salon. This person, again not my client, was the type that would bring her own coffee in a thermos. This was something she did every week when she came for her appointment. I think you must be surmising where I'm going with this.

She had a glass of wine, a little cheese, some of her coffee, a few crackers, and then some more coffee. By the time she got out from under the dryer she could hardly walk. You just have to picture a little old lady laughing and slurring her words, acting like a teenager after their first taste of alcohol, freedom at college. I knew it wasn't just the wine. I then checked her coffee thermos and whew! The liquor smell would knock you out. The combination of wine, liquor, and heat from the hair dryer. She was hammered. We somehow managed to keep her in the salon for quite a while, fed her lots of water and food, then when I knew should could walk and talk normally, I had her stylist drive her home and returned her car the next day. I have to admit she was funny and she was having a grand ole time for herself. It's amazing how some people can only show their fun side with alcohol. That fun side should be there all along. She is a sweet lady and I'm glad she was okay with what happened and felt she could return to the salon, without the thermos of course. We never served wine and cheese again.

CHAPTER EIGHTEEN

Survival Part III: I Beat Cancer

Look Good Feel Better is a charitable organization. It is based on the premise that if you look good, you will ultimately feel better. Makes sense. The program was comprised of the Cosmetic Toiletry's and Fragrance Association now known as The Personal Care Products Council, the American Cancer Society and the National Cosmetology Association now known as The Professional Beauty Association. Together they offered free classes for people who are going through the rigors of cancer treatment. As a past volunteer for this program and also an ovarian cancer survivor, I fully understand the importance of the program and more importantly the value of all the volunteers. It was a wonderful experience to watch a person who did not have hair including eyebrows and eyelashes as a result of chemotherapy be transformed into a smiling human being again. My best memory of one of these classes was of a young girl who, in the beginning of the class, wore a baseball cap and kept her head down. By the time we finished the session, the smile on her face was the most incredible sight to see. She was able to see a slight hint of eyebrows and skin that didn't look like paste. Even wearing a baseball cap made her look beautiful again. And yes, her head was now held high.

It was also healing for me to be a part of this transformation. I remember sitting at the end of a long table, women on both sides of me watching as all of the volunteers explain how to wear wigs and how to apply make-up without looking like you just stepped out of a circus tent, and more importantly, that they are not alone in this battle. What those women didn't know was not only was I one of their stylist volunteers but also a cancer patient and also bald.

The room was buzzing when I removed my wig to show them that I was one of them. Wigs don't have to appear fake. Not like they did back in the day and make-up can be applied tastefully. There are also many other options for comfort like scarves and terry cloth head wraps. To be honest with you, from my own experience, the wigs weren't always easy to wear all day long. Your head can become sore just from the hair loss but there is most always a solution.

When you get that diagnosis of the *big* C word, your world doesn't have to stop turning. Yes, you can feel sorry for yourself, who has a better right, you can be angry as hell at everyone and even at no one at all. Let you feel all of these emotions and then put your life experience to work. Talk about it, tell people you have cancer, let others know that they are not alone, and don't be afraid to show your bald head.

My own cancer diagnosis has helped me to help others not only through the past volunteer work but at my salon as well. There have been many times that I had to shave someone's hair off because of chemotherapy. Sometimes the hair would fall out in spots and would look a lot better completely shaved. The good thing was that I was able to connect with these women; they knew my story and, being a survivor of baldness and of cancer, gave them hope.

The families of the patients are suffering through this just as much. Many men have come to the salon with their wives or girlfriends, for moral support. I remember one young couple; they were so scared of the whole process when they came in that you could see the tears in both. Cancer frightens everyone. I have to say the men were extremely encouraging. No matter how old the patient and I have had people in their forties to eighties. The men always tell their spouse, "You look beautiful no matter what." So many of the men would ask me if I would shave their heads as well. I did. I never charged a cancer patient for shaving their heads nor the spouse. It was the only way for me to say, "I'm here, I've been there, and I'm sorry you have to go through this, but you are not alone."

It has been twenty years since I was diagnosed, hard to believe. I am lucky to be here and thank whoever is up there for allowing me be to be alive. I thank my loyal clients for sticking with me through those tough times, for always wanting to check under my wigs to see the progress of my hair returning. Also for asking me questions about my cancer because I never wanted that to be a taboo subject in the salon. I thank my family, especially my remarkable husband, Al, and our fantastic daughter, Crystal, for being there through all of the ups and downs of life. I love you both.

Sometimes it's just great to say, "So what if I have cancer? I'm not dead yet."

Don't you agree?

CHAPTER NINETEEN

Weddings

I'm going start by making a suggestion here. Brides, please confer with your attendants before you call your stylist. Make sure all of them are willing and able to make an appointment with the stylist long before the wedding day. They do not have to come in together as long as they come in ahead of time. This is called a trial run, a very important appointment. This gives us an idea of how you want to look and also gives us the opportunity to assess your hair. Will it be the right texture? Is it too curly or too short? What products will I need to accomplish the look we are trying to achieve? Also if you are to wear any kind of hair ornamentation such as a barrette or flowers and so on, please bring it with you. If that is not possible, bring a photo of this object so I am able to envision where to place the object in your hair on the day of the wedding. This trial run gives us an idea of how long it will take to get you out the door on the big day. One other thing, brides should tell their bridal party, "Yes, you have to pay your stylist for this trial run appointment." It's not free. If they are unwilling, then the bride should find a way to pay, either before their appointment or arrive with the group to pay at the appointment. The only other option: find new attendants. You are also expected to see to it that everyone pays the hairdresser for their hairstyles the day of the event as well. I don't know what happens to common sense in this matter. Do people really believe that we should take the loss for our time and talent? Should they not even blink an eye as they try to walk out the door? Were they not taught etiquette of any kind? Maybe that's a good subject for one of these bridal shows. Personally, I have never charged a bride for her big day hairstyle. That's just my gift to her but I never mention that until I'm ready to send her on her way.

You would not believe the wedding parties that have walked out of my salon assuming that the bride took care of the bill. Very uncomfortable chasing people on their way to the car, and in so many cases, they didn't even have money with them. Either they thought it was free or, well, damned if I know.

Throughout my journey, I've come across all kinds of bride issues. Not all were bad but yes there were a few "Bridezillas" along the way. I don't think that's a real name for a bride because my spell check has underlined it and no word to replace it so, but it really has a place in our visions of what brides can become while under stress, how they can lose all focus on the real meaning of the day. How they forget the reason for marrying is love, not how much it cost or what everyone is wearing or how they look. I wish they could see, the groom asked her to marry him not for all this other stuff that happens, but to be with her for the rest of their lives. The party and everything else is the bonus to it all.

CHAPTER TWENTY

Four Generations, Two Weddings

This tells you how long I worked at my career. I could not believe that, when I retired, an important milestone had taken place. I had the privilege of being the hairdresser to four generations of one family. How cool is that? This woman actually became one of my good friends; her mom had come to me at different times during my career. That's how I came to meet her. She loved to listen to stories of the parties I would have and mentioned on several occasions that she would love to be part of that fun. I finally asked her and her husband to come to one of the picnics, and from then on, we remained close friends. I've cut their children's hair and finally the grandchild's just before retiring. So I did the grandmother, mother, three daughters, and a grandchild. Actually, the grandson didn't sit still very long so I'm not sure how much actual hair got cut, but the thought was there.

First Daughter

The first wedding for the family was a quiet affair. The couple didn't want a big hoorah; her dress was lovely but no veil. This bothered me because the dress required something to make her stand out as a bride. The bride was getting dressed at one of the other family member's home because of a power outage. How awful was that? Not much anyone could do, but I'm guessing it put a damper on her spirits. I knew where the home was so I decided she needed something for her hair and a much-deserved boost of confidence. I went to the local florist and asked this wonderful designer and owner of the shop, if she could suggest something that wouldn't look too overdone but tasteful. The event was happening in an hour.

Although she was in the middle of speaking to a prospective clients' wedding party, she said she would come up with a plan. She then asked the other clients to have a seat and look through the floral design photos for ideas for their upcoming event and then started to pick flowers out of the case and pull together a very beautiful flower barrette for me to take to my friend's daughter. It was just what this beautiful bride needed. Her face lit up and the smile appeared. My point here is that even though this was to be a small immediate family-only wedding, the bride should always feel special and I believe she did.

Second Daughter

The next wedding for this family was a lot more involved. She had a large wedding party and it was held in a different state. Thankfully, Al and I were invited to the affair, which required overnight accommodations. I was thrilled to have had a room reserved for us, and happy to be able to bring all that I need in supplies to take care of the hair for the day. I styled a few of the guests that day and the mother and father. The bride, of course, is the star at any wedding and my number one priority. Luckily I had practiced this elegant look not only on her several times but also would do it on a mannequin a few times. She lived out of state so this was the best solution. It required a lot of hairpins and a ton of little white pearls along with—I can't begin to tell you how much—hairspray. She was very pleased with the result and never lost a pearl the entire evening. Well, she did but that was at the very end of a long and dance-filled reception. It always helps to have your stylist on deck for the big day in case of hair "meltdowns." Any mother of the bride knows what that word means.

At her bridal shower, I presented her with a photo of me holding her in my arms outside of the salon I had worked at. She was dressed for Halloween and so was I. What a precious moment for all, especially for me. Brings tears to my eyes even to this day. She now has several children of her own.

Third Daughter

There is a third daughter. I didn't have the pleasure of doing her hair for her wedding because, by the time she was ready to be married, I was too old of a hairdresser and she had been going to a younger salon for quite some time. I certainly understood. Oh, and by the way, it was her child that made this a four-generation chapter.

CHAPTER TWENTY-ONE

A Timeless Recipe

I would like to share with you a recipe that I have given to a few newly wedded couples over the years. Some changes have been made over the years, but that's what recipes and marriages do over time, they change. Enjoy.

A Loving Marriage
Ingredients:

2 People (doesn't matter race, religion, color, or gender)
2 Cups of devotion
6 Cups of understanding combined with an equal amount of patience
1- Pinch of mystery
2- Heaping hearts full of love
Add a whole lot of passion to taste

Combine all ingredients

Blend well

Allow to simmer for a lifetime (especially the passion)

When you think the recipe is done, check all ingredients.

You may need to add a little something! XXX OOO

CHAPTER TWENTY-TWO

The Wedding Challenge

Mothers and daughters have a unique relationship. I didn't say whether that is a good or bad thing because any mother knows, at any given moment, that relationship can run amok. This is true when it comes to planning a wedding with your baby girl. Why do we get so stressed out during this event? I just thought of something. What if we approach it with the same concept as I did while writing this book? We could think of it as eating an elephant; you can do it if you take one bite at a time. By the way my thanks to that instructor (the one that taught the class on writing and selling your book). She has amazing insight.

Our daughter's wedding was one of the most important days of her life and ours. I knew from the start that I would have to behave myself and not try to control all aspects of this journey. Anyone in my family will tell you that I do have a little bit of control issues. Maybe you shouldn't ask them, now that I think about it. Crystal and I have, for the most part, gotten along incredibly well through the years, but I think that was in part because of her respect for me as her mother. Yes, there were lots of times when we didn't see eye to eye on things. What parent doesn't lock horns with their children now and then? Okay, so it was a little more. My point, I couldn't have been that bad because she turned out great.

My husband and I were married in a court house with only our attendants, so it was difficult not to go overboard with our daughter's wedding. I had to keep telling myself it's Crystal and Jeff's adventure.

I had asked my sister-in-law to tell me when I was being a pain in the ass. I did not, under any circumstance, want to take away Crystal's time in the spotlight. Believe me I had a lot of input into this special time, but I think she was glad for my ideas and it was great fun. So that's my advice, try not to be a pain in the ass.

One of Crystal's requests was that I do only her hair for the wedding day and not her attendants'. She didn't want anyone with her either, just her and I at the salon. I couldn't believe how hard it rained that day. I remember her starting to cry, and then all of a sudden, she paused and said, "You know, Mom, I can't do anything about the damn weather [actually she used more to-the-point language] but I'm going to have a great time." She never shed another tear that day. Now I'm not so sure about the bag piper we hired to play as people were entering the church.

Have you ever seen a grown man in a soaking wet kilt? No one informed him before we arrived at the church, not to play in the rain. I think he may have shed a few tears.

It took four golf umbrellas to cover her gown while getting into church. Even the priest had mentioned that he could not believe the amount of rain. He then said to all of us that it was just like the song "Holes in the Floor of Heaven" by Steve Wariner and Billy Kirsch, and those rain drops were tears of joy raining down from those people we had lost and letting us know they were there on her wedding day. I felt that was a really nice thing to say.

While sitting in the pew waiting for her to come down the aisle, I said to myself I was the disciplinarian for her whole life. She always thought Daddy can do no wrong. I think he only raised his voice to her once in her life. I saw her through, like all mothers do, the heartaches of growing up, I taught her how to act in public, taught her to be polite (well, both of us did that). I did all the other things that mothers do. But, like so many others, she will always be daddy's little girl.

What I want to know is after all that mothers do for their daughters, why does the father get the glory of walking her down the aisle? I do have to admit they looked perfect together. He was so proud, head held high, looking like he just stepped out of a *GQ* magazine. Handsome as hell in is double-breasted tuxedo, arm in arm with the beautiful bride and taking that important stroll. The bride was beaming, looking toward her husband to be and yet holding on tight to her dad. Oh well, such is life. These days both parents can do the honor. Now that's a nice and well-deserved change, even though in hind sight I probably wouldn't have changed a thing.

There are so many emotions that occur before, during, and after a wedding if we would just learn to not get so wound up in all of it and just breathe and have some fun. We all need more fun in our lives. Dance!

CHAPTER TWENTY-THREE

Taking the Next Step

About seventeen years or so before I retired, I sold my first salon and decided to open one without any other stylist on board. I had grown tired of the drama that occurs when you have four other women with you. These people were not my employees. They were booth renters, which makes a huge difference when you are the owner. I understood that it was my responsibility to care for the salon in general and assumed the renters would care for their space, and some did. Others did in their own way I guess, just not to my standards. You see I have always had a thing about clean. For years my nickname was the white tornado. These women were my friends. They were at my house on weekends, often with their families and sometimes their friends as well. I had the swimming pool and big yard. I would even book a hall once a year to accommodate all of us around Christmas. I should also add that this included our own family as well. We're talking, at some events, eighty to a hundred people, maybe more. Gets real expensive really quick, and these functions were always funded by Al and me. We never asked anyone for a dime. The hall was free because we belonged to the club but DJs and food are not. So I guess in the scheme of things I expected more of these women. Anyway getting off track a little bit.

Over the years I have frequented many salons and I am disappointed in the cleanliness in some of these places. I know that not all salons are like this but believe me there are some that make me cringe. I really don't understand how you can work in an environment that makes you look less professional, no matter what that profession may be. Al and I were both tired of spending our weekends cleaning the salon only to have the girls tell me we shouldn't be touching their stuff. I can understand that. What I do have great issues with is hair stuck to the counters from so much hairspray and disinfectant jars that housed combs, which looked as though they . . . well, anyway.

After a while the friendships began to wane for lots of reasons. I accept the blame for a lot of the issues we had but not for all of it.

I was excited to have found a buyer for the salon and I had earlier informed the girls that I no longer wanted to own it; instead, I wanted to rent like they did. I even offered to sell to any one of them. No takers. The new owner took over and a very short time later all of the stylists decided to leave and rent somewhere else. They never once mentioned this to me until they had made the decision; once again it really was none of my business. I don't have the right to tell anyone where to work. It did, however, put this woman into a financial nightmare. That was something I do have a problem with, at the very least they could have arranged a meeting with the new owner to see if issues could be resolved. The owner of the building thought I should do something to help her, like what? I felt horrible but what did he expect me to do, buy it back? I was put out of work as well because she couldn't keep it afloat without renters. I went to work nearby for a very short period of time then opened the second salon, this time by myself. Nice break.

I learned some valuable lessons during that time with the girls. Number one, you can't buy your way into friendships. I think I was doing that all along. Number two, I'm not cut out to be in charge of anyone, and certainly not anyone's boss. I now know how it must have felt for the owners of all the other salons I worked at before I decided to venture out. The feeling of abandonment. My husband has always said that I think differently than anyone he knows, especially when it comes to common sense. That's where I might have gone wrong. I assumed it was common sense for everyone to stay at the salon even though I no longer would be the owner. I assumed it was common sense to keep the clients from having to go to a different location. I assumed they would think like me. Also I was foolish to think I could change anyone else when, in fact, all we can do is change our own way of thinking toward others. Sometimes I remember this lesson; other times not but I'm working on it.

CHAPTER TWENTY-FOUR

Self-Centered
Part I

Along the road to my future as a retired person, I encountered a few people who had all but forgotten I'm human. Just don't understand how minds work sometimes. While working in my second salon, the one where I worked alone, I had an episode of low blood sugar. I had done a finger stick on myself to test my numbers and managed to take a sip of juice. The next thing I remember is waking on the floor with a paramedic standing over me with an IV tube in my arm and a wicked headache. My husband was towering over me as well. It seems I passed out before I could get enough orange juice in me. My next client had come in and saw me on the floor and, knowing I was a diabetic, called 911 and told them I had attempted the juice and test kit was on the counter. I am so thankful for this woman;

she saved my life. A little side note here; people, please let others know of your illnesses wherever you work for all our safety.

Continuing on, I called this lifesaver client to thank her when I returned from the hospital. I offered to do her hair for free, the very least I could do. She proceeded to tell me what happened when my next client arrived during all the commotion. Apparently, this woman sat at the sink watching what was going on and waiting. She was very upset, not because I was on the floor, but because I wasn't going to be available to do her hair. I'm surprised my life saver didn't strangle her on the spot. Once again I thanked my lifesaver and dialed the other client.

I started by apologizing for any inconvenience I caused her, and before I could offer to do her hair for free, which still felt like the proper thing to do, she decided to tell me off. How she had to find someone else to cut and set her hair and she wasn't happy about it. This is the truth, not one single mention of what happened to me, or even if I was all right. I stopped her from saying anything else and told her I was glad she could find a hairdresser on short notice and that it would be a good idea to continue to see this new stylist. Click.

CHAPTER TWENTY-FOUR

Self-Centered Part II

Does your status in life make it okay to be a mean, nasty SOB?

When I think of this next client I am of two minds. On one hand, I understand, if your spouse is cheating on you, I certainly can see how that would affect your personality to some extent. On the other hand, was she mean before this rumored affair? This client was the wife of someone well known in our area. Someone that had long been known for his extracurricular activities. This gave her no excuse to be mean to anyone but him. If the only way that you can get through life is to think the world should bow at your feet, because of your personal problems, then that's a sorry and sad existence.

She was a weekly client and I treated her with great respect like I did all my clientele. I also knew she had some medical problems as we all do, but nothing major.

In the beginning she was fine; the other clientele actually thought it was great to be seen in the same salon, but then she gradually started making insulting comments about the other clients. Out loud. Things like:

"Does she know she looks awful in that style?"

"Is the stylist going to let her go out looking like that?"

"Does that manicurist ever comb that hair? It always looks messy!"

I wanted to say to her, "She's young and stylish. Not an old frump like you!"

She had an aide to assist her in getting to her appointments. This woman had to be a saint to put up with the comments. I myself let her get away with it too long. The clincher was the day she accused me of not paying attention to her because I left her under the dryer to process her color while setting another client's hair. I told her that I had her on a timer and would never neglect any client to take care of another. When I was finished with her appointment, she had the "balls" (no other way to put it) to tell me she was not going to tip me because I did another person's hair during her allotted time. I said to her, while trying my best to remain professional, "I never expect a tip from anyone." I made the next appointment for her, and then when it was quiet in the salon, I made a call to her and asked that she find another salon. I also told her that I felt hurt that she would say the things she did and that no salon owner expects a tip, nice if it happens but never should be expected. Also told her how she embarrassed me and the other clients, as well as the other stylist on a regular basis and could no longer accept that kind of behavior. I told her that I offered her a service in my salon for which I am paid but, under no circumstance, am I her servant. Do you know what she said to me? "Well, what do you want me to do, print a public apology in the newspaper?" I said, "No, I want you to find another salon." She then says, "Well, I already have an appointment with you for next week."

"You don't now."

I was actually shaking when I hung up the phone. I was nervous just thinking about the ramifications after refusing to book her another appointment or some other ridiculous thing she might do; strange thoughts I have. Talk about nerve. Should I have made better decisions when it came to letting her get away with poor treatment of everyone? The answer is yes. The other thing I did wrong was treat her differently than I would normally. I hate to admit that I was enamored by just having her choose my salon and that, my friends, should never happen. Another lesson learned.

With all these lessons learned, I should be a genius by now, don't you think?

CHAPTER TWENTY-FIVE

Halloween

Trying to outdo one another on Halloween in a salon was a tremendous challenge. One that required a great deal of thought as well as design technique. I've said many times that hairstylists are most often really good at design, not only with hair but with clothing choices, home décor, and floral arranging as well. I think it's because of having to know the good old color wheel. It's a must in the field. Floral design was going to be my second career but turns out I have allergies to a lot of flowers, not a plus on a resume to a florist.

Back to the costumes. The clients loved to see all of us dressed in full garb for Halloween. Everyone got into such a happy mode, clients included. Probably the most fun of any holiday we ever celebrated in salons was Halloween, and that was true in every salon that I worked. I remember the owner of the first salon. She came in with a grass skirt, a long dark black wig, big sunglasses, and under the grass skirt was a pair of panties with writing on them that said "I Got Leid in Hawaii." She obviously was more fun than any of us ever realized. I guess when it's your boss, you forget they are human beings and being our boss made it even more hilarious to everyone.

There were a few male stylists at this same salon, but this particular gentleman was quite the character. Made us laugh all the time. One year he went all out with his costume. It took quite a bit of thought and a whole lot of man-scaping, legs shaved, face, arms, but not the chest. You just have to imagine a guy over six feet tall with the look of a fur rug on his upper body. He wore nothing but a woman's black slip that was trimmed with lace. He also wore high heels and a blonde wig, tons of make-up as well. He also carried around a long cigarette holder with the cigarette. Can you do a visual in your head? He might have been re-born from another era. I don't know. One thing I do know is that I peed a little from laughing at him.

Another great costume (you may want to jot some of these down just in case you need ideas for your own costume party) was a court jester. This girl was the manager of a salon where I worked many years ago. No one can imagine the time it took to cut out all those triangles in red and gold felt and then sew them all together. Such imagination. It's not like any of us were getting paid to do this or winning any contest even. It was just for fun and some friendly competition. Amazing. We weren't the only salon that did this type of thing; a lot of them partook in the fun. The local news publication used to come to different salons and take photographs, which was very nice of them to do.

Some of my own ideas for Halloween were what I would call creative as well. One year I decided to dress like a HERSHEY'S BAR. I purchased brown felt, some silver fabric, and white tissue paper. I folded the fabric in half to look like a rectangle and then put two straps to hang from my shoulders. I added the white tissues at either end to replicate the white paper. I then cut out the letters from the silver fabric and glued them on. The next step was a hat that was a whole lot of aluminum foil in the shape of a candy kiss with a piece of tissue coming out of the top that said HERSHEY'S in blue ink. Everyone loves HERSHEY'S.

Another idea was dressing like a baby. I wore a white T-shirt with a large pacifier, attached with a very large safety pin that had blue ends. For the diaper, I cut up an old bed sheet. The funny part was making it real. The night before the big day, I put on the "diaper" and sat in a huge glob of yellow and brown mustard and let it dry overnight. Perfect! There were a lot of laughs for that one.

The nice thing about the fun on Halloween was that most of us stayed dressed when we went home so we could greet the trick or treaters. The parents were usually impressed and the kids thought we were funny, or maybe they just thought we were crazy.

CHAPTER TWENTY-SIX

The Hand Off

Giving my daughter away, not to her husband but to another hairstylist, was indeed a hard thing to do. I knew that it would have been a tough thing for her to tell me that she wanted to go to a younger salon. She would have been right. I probably would have been crushed.

She has always been hesitant about trying new styles, color, cuts, or whatever the trend might have been at the time. When I would create these different looks on her, I could see that she was less than thrilled about it sometimes and yet would say nothing negative, but boy, all you need to see with girls is a look. Moms do you know the one I mean, the one with eye roll and maybe a little low groan?

Even though I suggested many times that she should try to find a new person to go to, she wouldn't. The reason: because she felt that she was betraying her mom. I am almost certain of that.

Crystal is a very unique young woman, heart of gold. She had and still does have a sense of what is the right thing to do. She absolutely would not hurt anyone's feelings intentionally, definitely not mine.

She mentioned one day that a friend of her husband's wife is a hairdresser. Really, in my heart I felt this was the time to have a talk with her. I said that she needed to make an appointment with this girl. I also told her that she wouldn't hurt my feelings and that she should find someone else even if it wasn't this person, because I was not getting any younger and that if something were to happen to me, she would be lost by never having another person touch her hair in her life. Everyone reading this please, just think for a moment, how hard is it for you to find the right person to be your stylist, the one you trust with your crowning glory, your hair? Am I right? She said of course that nothing was going to happen to me, which is what she always says. Finally, she agreed. I know it was the best thing to do for her and for me. I can relax knowing that she can rely on someone else. This person has been able to do things to Crystal's hair that I would have been afraid to attempt. She has made her look her very best and always on trend. I've met this person, and not only is she a sweetheart of a person, but she has a great deal of talent as well. One other thing I know is that she will be a great friend to my daughter no matter how the hair thing turns out.

Is it difficult when someone says to her "What a great haircut. Did your mom do that?" The truth is yes, it is difficult. Was it hard for me to hand my baby girl off to another hairstylist? Absolutely. Was I thankful that I could have that conversation with her? Absolutely. The reasons, it was the right time. It just was the right time.

CHAPTER TWENTY-SEVEN

Just Having Those Conversations

How many times have you said to your spouse, "We need to talk"? How many times have you said the same thing to your children? Never enough.

I have found that, quite often, parents do not want to admit to themselves that our teenagers have hormones just like we did. Difficult thing to deal with, wouldn't you say? I've listened to many stories over the years about our little darlings. I think what frightened me the most was that the parents were blind to what the children were doing. Right now I would think twice about raising a family simply because of the problems with gangs, bad drugs, guns, things that can kill them. I am thankful for having our daughter in an era that was just beginning to show the ugliness that is out there today. I'm not sure our child was ready to hear what her father and I had to say but she listened. We told her that if she thought she wanted to try alcohol, then take a sip right now with us watching. The same with cigarettes—have a few puffs. We all know how it felt to take that first drag off a cigarette, disgusting. You feel weak, you tend to choke, and you stink from it. Right? It's only cool if you take that first drag in front of your friends. The same goes for drinking beer and wine. Neither taste great your first time, and whiskey, well, that only tastes good if you cover it with juice or soda. So they would be more likely to consume more if the first time was in front of friends. They would want to be cool and fit in.

If it's not new . . . These days I'm sure I would be in all kinds of trouble for my way of thinking.

Anyway, she told us when she was in college how she could see what happened with the girls who had never been allowed to try these things at home. It was the old forbidden fruit scenario. She saw the results—heads hanging in toilet bowls, one girl lying in her own vomit on the bathroom floor. She could have died; she was on her back.

I know that college antics just like high school are a rite of passage. Everything settles down eventually. I've never been a traditional parent. I wanted her prepared. Growing up one of eight there is not much I haven't seen. As an only child, our daughter didn't have much to draw on except what we tried to teach her.

A few of the parents that were my clients would insist that their children didn't drink, didn't party, or for that matter didn't, experiment with sex either. I always encouraged her to not have sex, at least not with just anyone and that I preferred she abstain until she was much older. I also knew that she was dating, and no matter what we would like for our children, it's not always going to turn out that way. I told her if she ever thought she might be that involved with someone, please tell us—no consequences, so we could get her the right information and protection. When that day came, my heart sank. I remembered what we told her and then I set up an appointment with my gynecologist. I figured it was better that a doctor tells her what to expect and the whole birth control thing. Safety first. This way she got the correct information. No eye rolling and no tendency for us to scream at her.

The strangest part was telling my husband that she wanted birth control. My first thought was he was going to go through the roof. My second thought was he hated the guy she's dating. To my surprise he said to me, "Well, we always told her that, when she was ready, to come to us so she would know the right way to protect herself." Okay, who stole my husband? He wasn't happy about any of it but we had to follow through on our conversation with her. I did tell her not to be pressured by this guy; that it was her choice. Do I think she believed that? No, I do not.

I am really glad that we have always been able to convey a message to her that she can talk to us about anything. Same goes for today and she is in her forties.

As parents, I feel we should all be able to talk to our kids about real life. It's never going to be easy, but I believe it is a necessary part of our relationships with them and sooner than later. Who better to tell them that the world is a very scary place right now and we need to talk about it? Do you really want their classmates to tell them about drugs, sex, guns, and whatever else is out there? I keep going back to the statement I always use: we are not their friends; we are their parents. We can be whatever they want us to be when they are grown. No, we do not have to scare them to death but please keep the lines open. We cannot shelter them from all the bad things that happen these days, and unfortunately, they can no longer be just kids in their teens. So I feel it is up to us to protect them by letting them know they can trust us to give them the right information and lend an ear at any time. No matter what the topic. These are just my thoughts.

CHAPTER TWENTY-EIGHT

Bucket Lists

Do you have a bucket list? I think we all do to a certain extent. We may not call it that but it seems to me that everyone wants to do at least a few things before the time comes to sit in a rocker, nosh on your toothless gums, and bitch about politics to anyone who will listen. That last one we do after we turn maybe fifty or sixty. Before that age, we have way more important things to worry about.

A client of mine had the right idea—do whatever you can feasibly do while you are young. Things you can afford of course. She had been with me a very long time, had a great family. The children were raised to be freewheeling think-out-of-the box people. I'd guess they were raised more like the old seventies hippy way, if you know what that means. Good for them, I say. One, I believe, is very good in the field of sports; another, very much into theater and the arts. Whatever the venture happened to be, she supported them all the way. She was the first mom I ever knew that accepted her son as gay publicly. Remember, the era was maybe early eighties. Not a lot of people were talking about it then. I loved her forward thinking. Nothing ever seemed to bother her, especially social status. It surprised me in the beginning that how she dressed for events was not a priority. Her husband, being in a field that required them to both attend functions, didn't seem to baffle her at all. Fashion wasn't her thing. She always felt if you don't like me for who I am, then that's your loss. Great attitude. I sometimes wondered if that was a smoke screen for the social insecurities.

A few years before, I retired she came to the salon for her weekly appointment and told me she had cancer. It was not something that I didn't already suspect. She was a very heavy smoker and I could see the weight loss and, of course, hear the dreaded cough. Through it all, she kept her sense of humor and always talked to me about what was happening to her. I was always glad that my clients felt they could talk freely to me about cancer. Not everyone can say what they want about the disease because most are trying to make it easier on the people they are leaving behind. I asked her one day near the end, is there anything that you regret or feel you haven't done in your life?

Her answer: "There is only one thing that I haven't done on my bucket list. I never did get to jump out of a plane."

I'll bet if she had a little more time she would have done that too. I miss her.

If you do have a bucket list, I say never let it get too short, keep adding wonderful things you want to do or things you want to say. I truly had some interesting clientele over the years.

CHAPTER TWENTY-NINE

Destiny

I would like to ask you, the reader, do you believe we are born with a set destiny? Have our paths been put in place long before our birth? It's something to ponder a bit.

I can recall as a little girl, sitting on the back of our sofa playing with my dad's hair and then brushing my mom's while we watched television. Of course I did not begin to think about what that little scenario would mean later in my life. It was one of those rare moments when there was no yelling at each other or beating up on one another. There was no alcohol-infused anger. So I would answer that question with a resounding maybe. After all, who's to say, but I'm guessing that destiny just may have had an effect on my choice for a career. Or maybe it was my parents' unknowingly guiding me to make the choice.

CHAPTER THIRTY

Are You Bored Yet?

I know it's a possibility. Right about now you're saying to yourself, "Enough already." I hope that's not true. I've tried not to be the writer that describes the flowers in a wallpaper pattern just to have a higher word count. And to take up space. I've also tried to blend each chapter with meaning to the next.

I do feel that what I have written is important. All of us need to make sure we have a little more respect for those people that offer us a service.

For example, the newspaper delivery person. They get up in the wee hours of the morning to put those newspaper sections together, especially on the weekends when all the flyers arrive. On days when the weather is poor, they also have to place everything in plastic bags to protect our treasured coupons. So please try not to blame them when your delivery is a little late. It's not always their fault. Sometimes the people that bring the sections to the delivery points are not on time either, for a number of reasons. But the one that takes the heat, of course, is your delivery person. I do know that I have a real gem and I make sure she knows how much she is appreciated.

The mailman. I have a special bond with these hard-working men and women; my husband was one of them for thirty-four years. They often take the heat for mail not arriving on time. Do you know that the mail comes to the post office pre-sorted to the routes? The carrier then takes it to his assigned streets. Do you also know the carrier does not determine which street to deliver first and which one is last? These people not only deliver your packages and letters; they also look out for you. If your mail hasn't been picked up on a regular basis, they will look into why. Do you realize that the only interaction some of our seniors have with another human being is with the letter carrier? They want to talk a little bit about their illnesses or how good of a golfer they used to be or about their children and that is okay—for the carriers that I know anyway. My own husband would talk to these people for as long as he could without running late on his route. Not easy to do but I believe it was part of the job and also who he was as a letter carrier that cares and an all-around good person. If the weather was poor, he would ring the bell and hand the person their mail so they wouldn't have to venture out on icy sidewalks or driveways.

You really can't ask for more than that. So please take a minute or two to thank the people that offer you any service and, yes, even your hairstylist.

CHAPTER THIRTY-ONE
Lives Intertwined

Have you ever thought about how our lives can intertwine, even years after the initial meeting or event? We really do seem to come full circle. Think about your own life for a minute. Has this happened to you?

Before I was married, I was hired for a job as a live-in nanny to three boys—ages three, five, and seven. I shouldn't judge, but their mother decided that being married to the father of these three beautiful boys was not in her life plan. She thought it would be better if the father kept the boys and she would have visitation rights. Actually, she had met someone at her office that had bigger aspirations for life than her husband had. In hind sight, she made the right choice with the children. I feel they were better off living without a mother that was unhappy. I do not know how she could leave the children or why she even had three, but that's just me I guess.

I became very close to the boys and had told their dad not to even think about anything happening between the two of us. (I was young and pretty and had a body at the time). As it was, living under the same roof was going to cause a lot of gossip. It was the late sixties.

It was a great job. I had my own room and I was free to do as I wish on weekends. The only downfall was I grew attached to the boys. This was what I wanted in my life—children, a nice home, just not their father as a husband. At one point, I thought about him and decided not a good match even though he was a terrific father and all around good guy. Just not for me.

While I was living there, I met one of the neighbors, Margie. She was older than me, but also had two little boys the same ages as my new little family. We got to know each other pretty well, did our ironing together at times, watched television late at night, having snacks and laughing at Johnny Carson. We also would stand with the children at the bus stop. Her in-laws lived next door to her so I got to know them as well. Everyone said the father-in-law was hard to be around, not the friendly type. Personally I had no problem with either of them. I got along with both of them just fine. He was origi-nally from Canada, a retired tough old lumberjack. What's not to like? Sometimes you just have to take the initiative and make your way into their lives. I have never been afraid to talk to people and I have found once again after our first hello, just ask them to tell you anything about their life. People love to talk, especially seniors. Too often we forget that they have a lot of experiences and general life lessons to tell us about. Take a few minutes to make their day. It might just make your day as well.

One day I saw an ambulance at Margie's in-laws home, so I ran over to see what happened, it was just a minor mishap. Thank God, nothing serious. While I was standing there with my new friends, a young man pulled into the driveway, looking a bit stressed. It seems that he left work because there was a shooting that had occurred in the office building where he worked. Three women were killed, then I believe the shooter killed himself in the stairway. One of those women was a girl I hung out with at a local bar from time to time. Very sad indeed.

Turned out that this young man was my new friend Margie's oldest son. I knew she had two older boys, just never met either one of them. It may sound strange to you, but I knew at that very moment when we met, he would be my husband one day. Yes, my new friend Marge was about to become my mother-in-law. Lives do intertwine.

I was still working at this very same live-in nanny job when a woman came to the door one day. She asked if she could take photos of the home and the barn across the street. She explained that she was a historian and this home where I lived was of great interest to her. It was very old—stone front, beautiful woodwork on the inside, and an old falling down barn. I don't know how long it had sat there unused but it was in tough shape. It's been taken down now but the house still remains. Anyway I called the owner and asked his permission before allowing her photo shoot. She was thrilled and thankful. I didn't see her again until many years later. I had opened my first salon by then. I walked in one day as she was having her hair done by one of the other girls. For years, she went to this stylist assuming that she was the owner of the business. When she found out I actually owned the salon, she wanted to come to me instead. I'm not sure why. I certainly knew the other girl was a much better stylist. That's not my insecurities talking; it's just a fact.

After taking care of her hair care needs for quite some time, I finally told her that we had met many years before during that photo shoot. She did remember the home, but not me. Why would she? I not only looked different, but had a different name. We talked about way back times and about her latest endeavor as an author. I was excited for her and her new book. I have to say I really don't know a lot about history, yet I still asked her for a signed copy when it was published. It was also another link to past and present. She and her husband eventually moved to a senior community that housed its own salon. Before she left, I got my signed copy. Who would have thought that one day I would meet her again after our first hello and would someday have my own aspirations of being an author? I truly enjoyed this person. She was so very smart and a pleasure to have in the salon.

I told you paths cross and lives intertwine. Remarkable, don't you think?

CHAPTER THIRTY-TWO

Real Estate (Maybe a New Career?)

If any of you have been in the real estate field, you already know what a challenge it can become. Shortly before giving up the salon, I decided with the encouragement of a friend to go to school to get my real estate sales person license. The thought was, I already had a pretty good list of clients to start with, and it might be something I could transition into after I retired.

Huge mistake. Well, not the school part. I don't think education of any kind is a waste. I passed the course with flying colors and obtained my license from New York State, good, right? My next move toward this new career was to find an agency in which to work. Your license must be held by a licensed broker. The person that encouraged me to give this career a try and myself went to work for a very small company. The first big challenge: I was still running the salon business. Now that is another lesson to heed. You just can't do it all and still remain a nice person. That might be just me but I should have waited for sure.

I was trying to do hair during the day as well as field telephone calls from people who wanted to know about property they were interested in purchasing. At night I would have to research listings, answer more calls, and still try to keep a clean and happy home. Thank goodness for Al. He was the most helpful person during that time. On weekends I would show properties or do open houses, which by the way is a very scary thing in real estate. You never know what kind of nut case is lurking, waiting for you to be alone in a home with no neighbors. My biggest problem with the whole real estate venture was, I thought that I had to be the mother to all. I had a very difficult time showing someone a home that in my heart I knew they couldn't afford. I know it's not up to me. I really do understand. But when a young woman came to me and said she was approved for a large loan online somewhere and couldn't obtain a copy of the prequalified letter, the hair stood up on my neck, so to speak. I begged her to please call a reputable bank or loan company. Someone local. She finally did come to find out there is no way she could afford a home in the range that she was looking. My instinct was correct. She also had other outstanding debt and children to pay for, and that was something she neglected to mention to me and not my place to ask. The banker she spoke with encouraged her to come in for consultation on getting her debt paid down and for advice on how to go about saving for that dream home, something she can look forward to in the future. Thankfully, she understood that I was just trying to help her. It could have been taken in a much different way. That was just one episode. It is not up to me and there is a fine line between trying to help and just minding your own business. I just can't help it. One other thing that steered me away from this career was my obsession with clean. I will never understand how anyone can think their home is ready to be shown if it has odors or hasn't seen a mop or dust rag in a while. I scrubbed bathtubs along with cleaning counters and sinks and, yes, toilets. No one could ever accuse me of not putting a great amount of effort into trying to sell their home, or to buy one. I took that career very seriously. They call it due diligence. I would say once again above and beyond the call. God bless those who chose that as a career, at least most of them. Some are questionable.

Anyway real estate is not for me. I worked at it for a while a few years maybe, then let my license go. I don't regret that decision at all.

CHAPTER THIRTY-THREE

Customer Service: Where Did It Go?

It's just my opinion, and yes, I do have a lot of them. Customer service is taking a bad turn. I'm not sure why, maybe the internet shopping, or possibly communications skills not being part of the training process when being accepted for a job. Or perhaps it's the financial aspect. My worry is that the bottom line itself is becoming increasingly more important than a relationship with the people that are giving us this bottom line. We might need to take a step back to a time when the business owner cared about the customers, knew everything about the family, and understood the value of that return client. I understand that big box stores and internet shopping are important and that mom and pop is rare these days, but all of that being said, we still need to talk to customers even if it is not face to face. When we are fortunate enough to have that live interaction we should take full advantage of the moment, ask a few questions, help the person locate what they are purchasing, and make sure it's the right one for them.

In the salon, I tried retail for a short period of time. It just wasn't for me. Plus, it was too difficult to keep records in check with the other stylists selling as well. Like I said before, there are also too many products out there. I'd much rather teach a client how to wear their hair than sell them something I may not believe is necessary.

Not long ago, feeling bored with retirement, I decided to apply for a part-time job in a retail clothing store for plus size women. This is something I knew I would enjoy. I'm a plus-size woman myself and I'm well aware of the difficulties in finding clothing that makes you feel and look nice. By plus size, I mean I was a size twenty-four, so I know the ups and downs of trying to choose the right clothing. I am now a size twenty and working on the next size down. It's a very difficult task to try and be a normal size, and ladies, I do not mean what the magazines refer to as normal. I would be thrilled to be a fourteen someday, but realistically, a sixteen is more likely to be attainable. As I progress with the weight loss, I will probably change my idea of what that normal number is, but for now, it's one day at a time.

I was successful at getting the job. Unfortunately my feet and legs didn't think it was a good idea.

While there, I was asked, as part of the training, to watch a few videos that would explain the store policies and how to approach the customer, things to do when a customer walks in the door. Meet-and-greet type of thing. I certainly knew about customer service but the videos were a requirement. Nice to know that someone at corporate headquarters cares enough to make sure the staff is properly educated on retail sales.

I'm a true believer in telling the truth when it comes to plus-size clothing, which is one of the reasons I knew I would be good at the job. One particular case: A woman came in to find a dress for a special occasion. I was not her sales person but it bothered me to no end that this person was trying on clothing that, well, wouldn't exactly look good on a thin person. I do not care what anyone else may think. *Heavy women should not wear stripes that go around your body.* If someone tells you it looks good, they are lying through their teeth. What the hell is the matter with the designers and the buyers for plus-size clothing? I once asked a sales clerk in another store, "Why do you have to place striped shirts and skirts in a plus-size department? Her answer: "It's in style." Yeah, if you wear a size two. A salesperson a little closer to my age at the time was listening to the conversation. She apologized and said she agreed with me one hundred percent. She then told me the buyer for the department was about a size six. I wish that explained all the other stores that do the very same thing.

Back to the customer in the dressing room. She came out with this striped thing on. I was trying to be tactful as I'm standing off to the side of another sales person, looking directly at the customer shaking my head no. I guess that really wasn't tactful. I took it upon myself to get involved for two reasons:

my need to help and my desire for someone to be able to feel they can approach me and tell me something doesn't look right. It's hard enough to look decent. No one needs to blow smoke up my skirt just to make a sale.

She did find a very nice dress, but in the meantime, she also thought she looked good in another dress that hugged to her butt. Every dressing room should have a rear-view mirror along with a voice over system that says, "Take it off!" Once again we showed her the reason that style and the fabric did nothing for her. In the end she was very happy with the outfit we helped choose for her including jewelry and the ever important and sometimes ignored under garments

That's another pet peeve of mine, the right bra. It's bad enough to be heavy, now add big breasts. They really need to be hiked up, ladies. Sports bras may be very comfortable but have no place in your work or evening wardrobe. Very few exceptions. Once again my opinion.

Have you ever tried to wear a swimsuit that has a shelf-bra, whatever the hell that is? To me it's just a piece of fabric that doesn't even begin to cover the nipples, yet alone lift and separate the size 44 double Ds? In my case triple Ds. Swimwear is a nightmare for us anyway. I'm better off with a pair of shorts and a T-shirt, at least I'll have a bra under it. I know, I know, there are some swimsuits that have bras built-in but we still need to have more designers pay attention to cup sizes as well. Huge market out there for this. Anyone else agree?

This would have been the perfect retirement job for me had it not been for the sore feet and the varicose veins as a result of standing on them for thirty-five years as a stylist. Of course being overweight and diabetic didn't help either. I even tried orthotic inserts to no avail. In the long run, I spent more money than I made but the money wasn't the reason I wanted to work there in the first place. I know in my heart that I was right for the job, the people loved that I cared about how they looked even though I took way too much time with each one of them. Once again I learned far too much about their lives. It's one of those jobs where I could make a difference in someone's life. There are many charitable things I could do to make a difference in someone's life. I could volunteer anywhere, but I was looking for a job that had more laughter, happy stuff.

I spent the last thirty-five years taking on everyone else's problems (my own fault). It was time for me to feel good again. I really did love that job. Hated the computer cash register but I loved the people.

CHAPTER THIRTY-FOUR

We the Seniors

Yes, I have turned into a senior citizen. How the hell did this happen and when? I don't mean just the age factor because, in my head, I've always thought of myself as twenty something. The body, well, I know what happened to that. As you must have surmised by now, I'm not young, at this chapter I'm sixty-nine years old and very close to that seventy mark. I find I am turning into a crotchety pain in the ass. Do any of you find this to be the case in your life? Are you letting things annoy the crap out of you that you never once thought about before? Things like politics, the television reality programs, social media, this computer that I'm using to write my thoughts on. I have written a tremendous amount about the lack of common sense throughout this book, all of which has annoyed me for sure, but that wasn't age talking. It was very real and had nothing to do with how old I was at the time. This is very different. I would not have thought about listening so intently to a political debate while I was working in the salon, even though I probably should have. The reason being, you should never discuss religion or politics with clients. That is if you want to keep them. I guess I've always tried to avoid those two subjects.

Now I find I'm truly upset with what's going on around me. I am well aware of how quickly my mouth can get me into a lot of trouble but just feel I'm allowed to voice how I feel because I'm a "senior citizen" and that's what we do, like it or not.

One item on that list of annoyances is cell phones. Is it necessary for you or your children to be on them all the time? Can you go to dinner and leave the electronics in the pocket? I say pocket because it has become a safety net for all of us, myself included, for emergency purposes. Can you look at each other and carry on a conversation for more than a minute without the phone? I was at a family dinner one day. I looked around and saw several guests with their heads down looking at their devices and typing away. I know how difficult it is for a hostess to prepare food and create a friendly, fun atmosphere for any function so I opened my mouth. I said out loud, "Is the person that you are texting that important? If so, they should be at this table celebrating with us." I won't reveal the hostess's name, but I said she has gone through a lot of time preparing this meal and deserves to have our attention as well as the other people at the table. I felt the need to say something even though it was none of my business. That is what I call the right of being a senior citizen, but should be the right of anyone. Just my opinion.

Sometimes I feel we walk on egg shells wanting to say something but don't for fear of the ramifications. I don't understand how we have become a world of disconnected humans.

One of the many things I do even if it does embarrass my family, I will make a point of going over to a table at a restaurant that has a family with children and tell them how well behaved their children are and how proud they should be. So far the response I receive from doing this has been favorable. Who doesn't like to hear nice things about their children? I wish I had the nerve to tell the other parents, "Hey, your kids are rude and a pain and that is nothing to be proud of." But you can only go so far even as a senior citizen.

Cell phones are really not the problem. It is the person hanging over the top of them. Children should be taught that there is a time and place for their use; adults should know this automatically.

Some of our long-time friendships have been put in jeopardy because of this device. It takes so long to schedule an evening together and then to have the people you're spending time with disappear into the abyss of the cell phone makes Al & I very uncomfortable. It leaves us feeling like we're interfering or maybe that our company is not that important. I can usually joke my way around these situations, but it is getting more difficult. I believe we need to focus on the human factor once again. maybe take a little break from that world.

All of our electronic devices are considered wonderful technology and certainly needed in our everyday lives. We would be lost and out of touch with the world if we didn't have them. The question here is, do we really need them twenty-four seven? I guess that will have to be decided by each one of us. Whatever your answer may be, at least I've said my piece as a senior citizen. Oh crap, my cell phone is ringing. Be right back!

CHAPTER THIRTY-FIVE

It's Christmas Again

Yes, it has taken me through another holiday season to put these words on paper. During this time, I have had many thoughts about whether anyone would really understand why I wanted to take on this project and if anyone would actually want to read what I have to say. I believe my words have been well directed and that most, if not all, readers will make a conscious effort to see how not only my career but my life and that of any stylist can be changed by the words you say to us: after our first hello.

I do know that not all of us in the field of cosmetology really care about your life, but I'm going to guess that those are the ones that are more focused on themselves than others. Since retirement, I've been to a number of salons for my hair-care needs and have encountered several stylists who don't even know enough to say to a client, "Hello, my name is . . . How are you today?"—the most basic statement in any field of business. How very sad for them and for all of us. One can only assume that most of those people will not find a lifetime career in anything, not just cosmetology. You know, it's not only my field that is negligent in this. I have been observing people lately and I am surprised, although I shouldn't, be on the lack of etiquette. I may get into trouble for saying this, but believe I have to. Doctors and medical staff, hospital staff, and lots of receptionists in all fields. They just don't introduce themselves or say hello. Is it possible that the only business I have come across in recent months to say, "My name is . . . What may I get for you?" is a chain restaurant? I'm definitely not an expert on the subject of etiquette, but it just doesn't seem right. Anyone else feel the same? Once again common sense should be a requirement, but how do you teach the subject? Should it be taught at home from childhood? Is there a set format that we could use as a lesson plan? Damned if I know.

Christmas is a wonderful time of the year. It's a great time to reflect on years past and those who are so dear to our lives. I have to say, at this time, that I have been truly blessed in this life and not just stressed as parts of this book would indicate.

The time it has taken to write this has been a slow cleansing of the soul for me and a chance for me to heal by sharing my stories, my thoughts, my advice (not that anyone really wanted it) with you, and also by including you my reader along the way. I sincerely hope I have made you think about your own families, a little trip down memory lane perhaps. I also hope you were able to laugh a little as well, and a wish from me that you treat your stylist and anyone that offers you a service with respect. I also hope that any stylist reading this will, in turn, have great respect for the clients in their salons.

Another little notation. Stylists, please refrain from getting too involved with your clients' personal lives like I did, but then again, you never know what an amazing journey you might go on after your first hello.

CHAPTER THIRTY-SIX

Still Trying to Decide (What's Next?)

What do I want to do with my life next? To tell you the truth, I really don't know the answer to that question. What's ahead may depend on what happens with this book. Will it be what a publisher is looking for? Do I self-publish? Is it something that will require me to be available if it is marketable? Regardless, I will certainly finish what I have started because I believe I have something to say and my words may have made a difference in your life. At the very least, I hope it made you take a moment to reflect.

If by chance you are just a relative going through my stuff because I'm no longer mentally capable of doing so myself, then maybe it's about time you read what my life was like and you will gain a little respect for the career I once had. Either way, I'm so happy I took on this challenge.

Wishing you well.

Love, *Barbara*

ABOUT THE AUTHOR

The author is a licensed cosmetologist and former owner of two salons, a career that spans thirty-five years. She currently resides in a retirement community in upstate New York with her husband, Al. They have been married for forty-five years and are proud parents of one daughter, the absolute love of their lives.

CPSIA information can be obtained
at www.ICGtesting.com
Printed in the USA
FSOW01n2046310717
37097FS